THE FINGER LAKES

REGION OF NEW YORK

A PHOTOGRAPHIC PORTRAIT

PHOTOGRAPHY BY
KEVIN STEARNS

First published in the United States
of America by:

Twin Lights Publishers, Inc.
10 Hale Street
Rockport, Massachusetts 01966
Telephone: (978) 546-7398
http://www.twinlightspub.com

ISBN 13: 978-1-885435-56-8
ISBN 10: 1-885435-56-8

10 9 8 7 6 5 4 3 2 1

(right)

DUSK ON SENECA LAKE
WATKINS GLEN, NY

The crown jewel of the Finger Lakes, Seneca
Lake's natural beauty epitomizes the many
reasons why Finger Lakes country is the #2
tourist attraction in New York State. The
deepest and widest of the six major lakes,
Seneca Lake sits in the geographic center of
the Finger Lakes and provides a perfect
setting for lakefront living and world-class
fishing and boating.

Editorial by
Francesca Yates and Duncan Yates
http://www.FreelanceWriters.com

Technical Advisor
Sally Billen

Book design by
SYP Design & Production, Inc.
http://www.sypdesign.com

Printed in China

The Finger Lakes region of Central New York is one of the most stunning and studied natural settings in the world because of glaciers and 360-million-year-old rocks.

It is a mystical place where the Earth lets you in on its ancient secrets and tells you the story of how planetary forces began to sculpt its surface two million years ago into the astonishingly dramatic landscape that enchants us today.

This photographic portrait celebrates the geology that has made this area world-famous. Page after page of images brings you deeper into Finger Lakes country as you follow paths through lush, hardwood forests, hike the winding, rim-side trails of deep gorges, and feel the cool spray of waterfalls as tall as 20-story buildings.

The melodious names of the lakes will begin to roll off your tongue—Canandaigua, Seneca, Cayuga, Keuka, Skaneateles, and Owasco—as you get a taste of life on these waters and in the quaint towns that nestle on the Finger Lakes' shores.

These photographs also honor an area equally rich in human history. It is the birthplace of the women's rights movement and the place where geology in 19th century America was studied and defined. It is where professional auto racing came into its own and where glass making became an art form. It is the place where a small, agricultural school became a top Ivy League university, and where people commune with nature every day because it is right at their doorstep.

Welcome to Finger Lakes country!

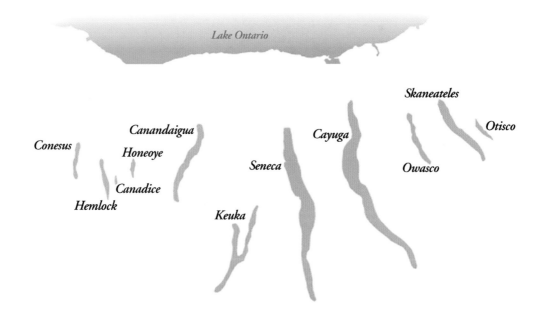

MIDDLE FALLS
LETCHWORTH STATE PARK (opposite)

The majestic geology of this popular state park has earned it the nickname, "Grand Canyon of the East." Over thousands of years of advancing and receding glacial activity, the Genesee River carved a deep gorge in the softer sandstone rocks, creating waterfalls along the way that rush over sheer rock cliffs. The 107-ft Middle Falls is the highest of the gorge's waterfalls.

ROWING A SHELL ON CAYUGA LAKE INLET (above)

This flat-water inlet on the longest of the Finger Lakes offers a leisure-ly, pristine four-mile row for skullers, and canoers. There is the con-venience of dock-side restaurants, bars, and an ice-cream shop for stops along the way.

FISHING AT FALL CREEK, ITHACA, NY (opposite)

Below the scenic Ithaca Falls, Fall Creek is an angler's paradise in summer when landlocked salmon and trout are plentiful.

WINTER VIEW FROM MCGRAW TOWER
CORNELL UNIVERSITY (above)

When the tower's splendid bell chimes ring out over the campus, even the coldest winter days can suddenly seem warmer. Every Valentine's Day, the chimes play the "Jennie McGraw Rag," in honor of the chimes' donor, who died soon after she returned home from her honeymoon.

ITHACA FALLS IN WINTER (opposite)

Ithaca Falls, the crown jewel of the Ithaca gorges, is spectacular anytime of year. Gazing at it, frozen solid and snow covered, you can still feel the power of this 150-foot waterfall.

9

INDIAN PIPE WILDFLOWER
FINGER LAKES NATIONAL FOREST (above)

Wildflowers grow in abundance in these dense woods. Nestled on a ridge between Seneca and Cayuga Lakes, Finger Lakes National Forest is an ever-changing canvas for visitors who follow the park's trails over gorges and ravines and through pastures and woodlands.

ROBERT H. TREMAN STATE PARK
ITHACA, NY (opposite)

The highlight of this wildly beautiful park is Enfield Glen, a deep gorge with a rushing stream that cuts between sheer cliff walls. The gorge's trails wind past a dozen waterfalls, often close enough to spray visitors on hot, summer days.

EZRA CORNELL STATUE
ITHACA, NY (above)

A mechanical engineering genius and a shrewd businessman who founded Western Union Telegraph Company, Ezra Cornell, the university's founder, envisioned a university where any person could find instruction in any study. He successfully promoted the idea to state legislators in 1865 and personally donated over $500,000 (in 19th century dollars). Today, Cronell is the largest of the Ivy's and a place where intellectual pursuits flourish.

MCGRAW TOWER
CORNELL UNIVERSITY (opposite)

The tower is famous for its bell chimes, a donation from heiress Jennie McGraw, daughter of lumber baron, John McGraw. Her father funded McGraw Hall, the Ivy League school's first building. Today the chimes' repertoire of 2,000 songs is a constant delight to the community.

SCHOELLKOPF STADIUM
CORNELL UNIVERSITY (above)

Schoellkopf Stadium is home to Cornell's Big Red football, lacrosse, and field hockey teams. After a $3.6 million facelift in 1986, the rejuvenated stadium set the stage for more home game victories over Cornell's Ivy League rivals.

FINGER LAKES NATIONAL FOREST (opposite)

Potomac Road winds through the Finger Lakes National Forest from Valois to Reynoldsville.

ST. PETER'S EPISCOPAL CHURCH
HOBART/WILLIAM SMITH CAMPUS, GENEVA, NY (above)

This historic stone church is an outstanding example of the English Gothic style. Completed in 1870, it was designed by Richard M. Upjohn, the renowned "father of English Gothic Architecture in America." Over time, the fine square tower was erected, and other enhancements and 20th century renovations created the current structure of this active Geneva church.

JOHNSON ART MUSEUM
CORNELL UNIVERSITY (opposite)

Cornell's Johnson Art museum, designed by I.M. Pei, houses one of the finest art collections in New York State and is recognized as one of the most important university museums in the country.

BROWNIE'S VEGETABLE STAND
JACKSONVILLE, NY (top)

In Finger Lakes country, stopping along the way can be as much fun as arriving at your destination, especially if you are buying fresh-picked fruits and vegetables from local farms.

SUNFLOWERS
CANANDAIGUA LAKE AREA (bottom)

Canandaigua is the Iroquois word for the "chosen spot," and the area is truly blessed with the spectacular scenery for which the Lake Country is known.

NEW ENGLAND ASTERS
HECTOR, NY (opposite)

Profusions of wildflowers, like this purple beauty, await you in the meadows and damp thickets of this idyllic national forest, which has the distinction of being the state's only national forest and the smallest national forest in the nation.

PINK LADY'S SLIPPER
FINGER LAKES NATIONAL FOREST (above)

Native Indians thought this attractive flower looked like a moccasin and believed that its mere presence induced spirit dreams. Today you'll find it in areas like in this shady, hardwood forest.

FOUNTAINS AT SUNSET
ITHACA COLLEGE (opposite)

At sunset, the fountains of Ithaca College seem to pay tribute to the majestic Cayuga Lake below. The town of Ithaca is amidst an unparalleled natural setting of lakes, forests, rivers, waterfalls, and gorges that make Finger Lakes country one of the richest geological areas in the world.

SQUIRREL CORN, MULHOLLAND
WILDFLOWER PRESERVE
SIX-MILE CREEK, ITHACA, NY (above)

This urban wilderness area offers miles of trails and delights visitors
with a rich forest, carpet of wildflowers as far as the eye can see.

SENTRY FALLS
WATKINS GLEN STATE PARK (opposite)

Sentry Falls is the first of 19 spectacular waterfalls that spill down
rock walls in just two miles of this famous glacial gorge. Above the
camera's view on the 52-ft-high Sentry Bridge, visitors can peer
through a hole where an 18th-century water wheel once powered
a grist mill.

TAUGHANNOCK FALLS
TAUGHANNOCK STATE PARK, TRUMANSBURG, NY (above)

People on the footbridge are dwarfed by the imposing 215-ft Taughannock Falls, cascading in a single, dramatic drop over a sheer cliff. This is one of the highest waterfalls east of the Rocky Mountains.

FISHING AT ITHACA FALLS
ITHACA, NY (opposite)

The beauty and tranquility of Ithaca Falls are enough to bring most people here, but fishermen have another good reason. In early summer, landlocked salmon and trout almost guarantee a good day's catch.

ROBERT H. TREMAN STATE PARK
ITHACA, NY (above)

Afternoon sunlight penetrates the park's lush forests and provides sharp contrast to a dark stone bridge across the Enfield Glen gorge that connects with winding trails throughout the park.

TAUGHANNOCK FALLS
TAUGHANNOCK STATE PARK,
TRUMANSBURG, NY (opposite)

Hiking trails offer stunning views of unique geological formations such as the majestic 215-ft Taughannock Falls. The park amenities include camp sites, cabins, boating, fishing and swimming on Cayuga Lake.

WATKINS GLEN STATE PARK GORGE (above and opposite)

Watkins Glen is the most dramatic and spellbinding of the Finger Lakes state parks. The main attraction is a deep gorge with a mountain stream that plummets 400 feet in less than two miles, creating 19 cascading waterfalls, and 300-ft shale and sandstone cliffs.

Park visitors walk along the spectacular gorge trail, with its 800 stone steps winding over and under the waterfalls. Some of the foot trails along the gorge were shaped centuries ago by Native American Indians.

ITHACA AND CAYUGA LAKE
ITHACA, NY (pages 30–31)

Overlooking Cayuga Lake, Ithaca is blessed with one of the most spectacular, natural settings in the world. The home of Ivy League school, Cornell University, and Ithaca College, with its fine music and theater arts programs, the town offers small city charm and big city culture.

BALLARD POND
FINGER LAKES NATIONAL FOREST (top)

Ballard Pond is one of 22 wildlife ponds in the forest. A popular spot for fishing and bird watching, it is stocked each spring with rainbow and brook trout to complement the native fish.

STEWART PARK
ITHACA, NY (bottom)

Every summer, young and old gather at this popular park to play sports, picnic and relax. On the shores of Cayuga Lake, it provides a panoramic view of the lake and surrounding hillsides—a perfect backdrop for memorable sunsets.

CASCADILLA CREEK
ITHACA, NY (opposite)

The trail along the Cascadilla Creek gorge conveniently begins in downtown Ithaca and rises one-third of a mile to the Cornell University campus. Hikers enjoy the quick and dramatic progression of six different waterfalls that culminate with Giant's Waterfall, the gorge's most striking one.

FINGER LAKES NATIONAL FOREST (previous page)

The last remnants of an ice storm passes out of the region in mid to late afternoon. As the sky opened up, the warm afternoon light lit the landscape revealing what nature had just created. Winter calls cross-country skiers, snowmobilers, and other outdoor enthusiasts to the area's 25 miles of trails.

WINTER ON SENECA LAKE
VALOIS, NY (opposite)

Even the coldest winter days won't stop an avid angler from dropping a line in Seneca Lake, the deepest and widest of the Finger Lakes. Every Memorial Day weekend, the National Lake Trout Derby is held here, celebrating its well deserved reputation for world-class fishing.

ICE CLIMBING AT TINKER FALLS
CORTLAND COUNTY, NY (above)

Twenty feet high, Tinker Falls is one of the smallest waterfalls in the Finger Lakes area. In winter, ice climbers find the frozen falls tall enough to be quite a challenge.

BEHIND TINKER FALLS
CORTLAND COUNTY, NY (opposite)

Visitors to Tinker Falls can walk inside the rocky tunnel behind the falls and enjoy this special "back-stage" view. The waterfall is an easy, short walk from the parking area.

SHINDAGIN HOLLOW STATE FOREST
CAROLINE, NY (above)

This large forest near Ithaca is shaped by two river creek valleys. The central hollow of the forest is a wide, gorge-like valley that comes alive every spring with vibrant, native wildflowers.

LICK BROOK GORGE
NEWFIELD, NY (opposite)

The Finger Lakes region is well known for an abundance of magnificent waterfalls including those at Lick Brook Gorge. Following the Finger Lakes Trail, hikers can reach all three of the gorge's cascading waterfalls.

ITHACA FALLS
ITHACA, NY (above)

Ithaca Falls is just one of many reasons why Ithaca is a popular destination for nature lovers. Unlike many wilderness waterfalls, this high
and wide "urban" waterfall is easy to reach and treats visitors to a
spectacular cascade rushing down a 150-ft cliff.

BUTTERMILK FALLS STATE PARK
ITHACA, NY (opposite)

Buttermilk Falls State Park takes its name from the foaming cascade
formed by Buttermilk Creek as it flows down the steep valley side
toward Cayuga Lake.

BUTTERMILK FALLS STATE PARK
ITHACA, NY (above and opposite)

The Finger Lakes region, in general, and Ithaca, specifically, contain some of the finest exposures of rocks known anywhere in the world from the Devonian Period (415 to 360 million years ago).

This park brims over with spectacular beauty and many ways to enjoy it all, with campsites, playing fields, picnic areas and a swimming pool. Miles of hiking trails wind through woodlands, meadows, wetlands and past the gorge's waterfalls.

MAPLE SUGARING
MUMFORD, NY (above)

As March days lengthen, the promise of spring stirs the juices in maple trees throughout Finger Lakes country. Visitors to maple farms and area museums can experience the art of maple syrup production, just as European settlers were taught by Native Americans centuries ago.

TAUGHANNOCK FALLS TRAIL (opposite)

A brisk, autumn day showcases the special magic and colors of a hardwood forest along the trail leading to the majestic, 215-ft Taughannock Falls.

SCENIC VINEYARD IN WINTER
HECTOR, NY (above)

When the snow melts in the Finger Lakes region, wine country comes
to life. Millions of grape vines in over 100 wineries on verdant, lakeside
slopes begin to grow the famous fruits that create award winning wines.

THIRSTY OWL WINERY
OVID, NY (above)

Under a fresh blanket of snow, vineyards paint a scenic winter post-
card. Thirsty Owl is the newest vineyard and winery on Cayuga Lake
and stretches out over 150 acres with 2,000 feet of lake frontage.

WINTER VINEYARD
HECTOR, NY (previous page)

A winter snow dramatizes the perfect symmetry of rows of grapevines in this Hector winery, one of 26 vintners on the shores of Seneca Lake.

DAWN ON CANANDAIGUA LAKE (above)

This fish-rich, glacial lake provides easy access for boaters from public launches at the north and south ends, as well as many private piers for its lakefront residents.

DAWN ON CANANDAIGUA LAKE (above)

It is easy to see why the native Seneca Indians called this area "Canandaigua" or "the Chosen One." One-and-one-half miles at its widest point and nearly 16 miles long, it is the fourth largest of the six, major Finger Lakes.

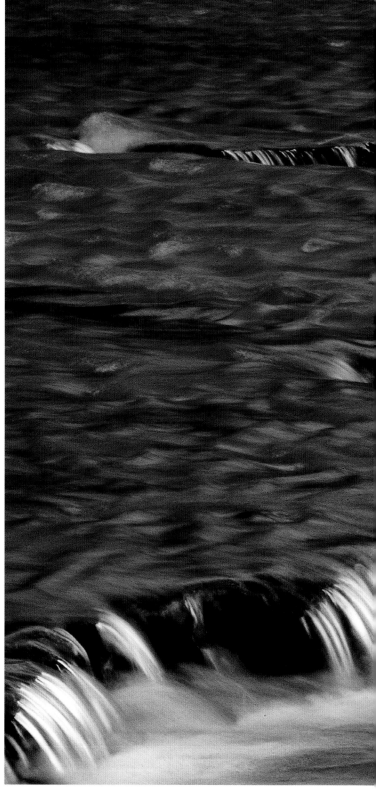

SUNSET ON SENECA LAKE (above)

Sunset is a magical time on Seneca Lake as boaters reluctantly return to shore, ending a perfect day on the largest of the Finger Lakes.

TOUGHANNOCK CREEK
TOUGHANNOCK FALLS STATE PARK (opposite)

Toughannock Creek flows through the breathtaking Toughannock Falls State Park in a series of discrete cascades and waterfalls. Over millions of years, the erosive action of the creek's waters has exposed 400-foot walls of shale and sandstone along the gorge trail.

LUCIFER'S FALLS
TREMAN STATE PARK, ITHACA, NY (above and opposite)

Plunging 115 feet over sheer, rock cliffs, Lucifer's Falls is the highest
and most spectacular of the three waterfalls in the park's popular
gorge. Climb a stone pathway up to the top of the Falls and see
through the woods to the lower park over a mile away. Park amenities
include camping, picnicking, fishing, swimming, and hunting.

SONNENBERG GARDENS
CANADAIGUA, NY (opposite)

Sonnenberg Mansion on Canandaigua Lake was formerly the summer home of benefactors Frederick Ferris Thompson and his wife, Mary Clark Thompson. The tour of its exquisite gardens begins at the historic Lord and Burnham Conservatory, one of the most important residential greenhouse complexes in the United States.

TRILLIUM WILDFLOWER
FINGER LAKES NATIONAL FOREST (top)

A drive through this unusual, national forest reveals a beautiful and diverse landscape of hardwood trees, abundant wildflowers, and fenced-in pastures where thousands of cows graze.

ORCHID SHOW
SONNENBERG GARDENS (bottom)

The Conservatory includes the domed Palm House (*opposite*) and other display houses that feature a breathtaking abundance of orchids, cacti, and lush tropical plants.

BUTTERMILK FALLS STATE PARK
ITHACA, NY (previous page)

During the 1700s, the native Cayuga Indians lived near Buttermilk
Falls in the village of Coreorgonel. There were twenty-five log cabins
surrounded by cultivated fields and plum and apple orchards. The
inhabitants abandoned the village during the turmoil of the
Revolutionary War.

SIX-MILE CREEK
ITHACA, NY (above and opposite)

Meandering in and around Ithaca, scenic Six-Mile Creek is also the
source of the city's water supply. A natural gorge separates the higher
reservoirs and the Van Nattas Dam from the waterfalls much further
downstream.

CANANDAIGUA LAKE (top)
This bucolic view looks south and down the east shore of Canadaigua Lake.

BARN ART MURAL
CANANDAIGUA LAKE (bottom)

The fields seem to stretch out forever behind this playful barn mural. Quieter now, Canandaigua was once the capital of a vast frontier that expanded westward to Buffalo. When the Erie Canal officially opened to the north in 1825, Canal cities such as Rochester became better alternatives.

GENESEE RIVER
LETCHWORTH STATE PARK (above)

It took 12,000 years to do it, but it was well worth the wait. Over
time, the Genesee River, one of just a few rivers in North America
that flow north, created a spectacular, deep gorge, complete with
three waterfalls, in the soft sandstone rocks of this famous state park.

MIDDLE FALLS
LETCHWORTH STATE PARK (above)

This popular trail winds along the gorge's rim and provides ideal, scenic lookout points. Here sightseers pause to enjoy the majesty and fury of the highest waterfall in the gorge.

CAVERN CASCADE
WATKINS GLEN STATE PARK (opposite)

Hikers on the scenic Gorge Trail are treated to a winding path that takes them behind one of the glen's major waterfalls. Over thousands of years, Cavern Cascade's waters have worn away shale rock in the cliff wall, creating this special view of the falls.

LETCHWORTH STATE PARK (above)

The early light of dawn greets the moor-like fog suspended between
the hills and gorge walls of this famous park. While hiding the beauty
below, the mist creates its own gauzy spectacle.

UPPER FALLS
LETCHWORTH STATE PARK (above)

One of three waterfalls on the Genesee River, the 71-ft-high Upper
Falls creates a wide cascade over the gorge's cliffs. Other intermittent
falls on the river's smaller tributaries flow in spring and temporarily
create some of the highest falls in the state.

ENFIELD GLEN AT ROBERT H. TREMAN STATE PARK (above)

The dappled afternoon sunlight finds its way deep into the gorge as visitors pause on a stone bridge to enjoy the gorge below and nature's splendor surrounding them.

JACK IN THE PULPIT, GREAT GULLY UNION SPRINGS, NY (opposite)

Wildflowers like this Jack-in-the-Pulpit love the damp woods, rich soil and running waters of the Finger Lakes gorges. They blossom in profusion along stream beds or forest floors.

CAYUTA LAKE (above)

The wider, panoramic scenery of the Finger Lakes region is created by
millions of perfect details like these lily pads floating on the flat
waters of Cayuta Lake. The Indian word "Cayuta" means "little lake."

OVERLOOKING UPPER FALLS
LETCHWORTH STATE PARK (oppositee)

Stunning birds' eye views like this illustrate why Letchworth is called
"the Grand Canyon of the East." Follow the park's seven-mile trail
along the deep chasm's rim for dramatic river and waterfall views, or
follow other trails that take you deep into dense, hardwood forests.

ITHACA FALLS (pages 74–75)

This happy couple, idyllically poised at the base of these powerful
falls, seems oblivious to the 150-foot wall of water behind them. This
urban waterfall is on the Fall Creek Gorge in Ithaca. The gorge path
climbs quickly past more waterfalls upstream on its way to the
Cornell University campus.

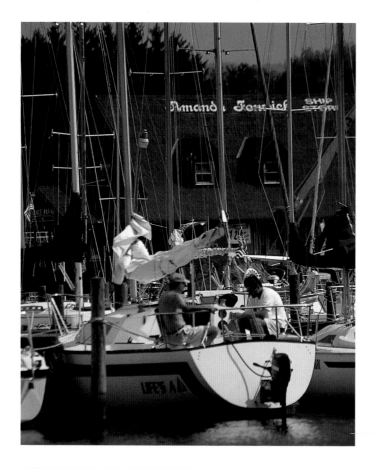

WATKINS GLEN MARINA (top)

On the south end of Seneca Lake, a sailor at Glen Harbor Marina prepares his sailboat for an adventurous day on the lake.

TOUR BOAT ON SENECA LAKE (bottom)

Captain Bill's Columbia, one of several tour boats on the Finger Lakes, offers dinner and lunch cruises, moonlight cocktail cruises, as well a romantic setting for weddings.

ALLAN H. TREMAN STATE MARINE PARK
CAYUGA LAKE (oppositee)

One of the largest inland marinas in the state, this marine park boasts of 400 slips, picnic areas, playing fields, and access to Seneca Lake and the Cayuga-Seneca Canal, 40 miles to the north.

THE MALABAR X TOUR BOAT (above)

When tourists and locals want a memorable sailing experience on Seneca Lake, they climb aboard the Malabar X, a recently restored, vintage, schooner yacht.

The Malabar X has a colorful past. Built in 1930 as a racing schooner, it won the prestigious Bermuda Race in 1930 and 1932. The 60-foot yacht was recently voted "One of the Top 100 Yacht Designs of All Time" by Yachting Magazine.

SAILING ON SENECA LAKE (opposite)

Prior to raising its sails, the elegant Malabar X motors out on Seneca Lake with a tour group on board. When the wind fills its jib and mainsail, this noble wooden schooner comes alive as its bow slices through the deep lake waters.

BICYCLING FINGER LAKES (above)

Public roads offer constantly changing, panoramic views of forests, gorges, waterfalls, rivers, valleys, hills and lakes.

TAUGHANNOCK FALLS
TAUGHANNOCK STATE PARK (oppositte)

A scenic walk through the park's dense, hardwood forest rewards visitors with a clear view of the spectacular, 215-foot Taughannock Falls, one of the highest waterfalls east of the Rockies.

BICYCLING FINGER LAKES (above)

Rich with spectacular natural beauty, the Finger Lakes region offers a thrilling ride for cycling enthusiasts, whether they are touring the countryside for several days or just out for a short ride.

FISHING ON KEUKA LAKE
HAMMONDSPORT, NY (pposite)

Wet a line in Keuka Lake, and you will soon see that the fishing is excellent from one tip of the lake to the other. Bountiful supplies of lake trout, small-mouth bass and land-locked salmon make delicious "catches of the day."

THE FOSTER COTTAGE MUSEUM
CLIFTON SPRINGS, NY (top)

Once the home of Dr. and Mrs. Henry Foster, this striking Victorian house is now home to the Clifton Springs Historical Society and a museum celebrating the village's unique history.

"JENNY," GLENN H. CURTISS MUSEUM
HAMMONDSPORT, NY (bottom)

After breaking air speed and distance records, Glenn H. Curtiss, the father of naval aviation, developed and flew the first flying boat prototype which he tested on Keuka Lake and produced for the U.S. Navy. Curtiss also produced the "Jenny," pictured here, one of 6,000 planes used to train World War I pilots.

VILLAGE CLERK'S OFFICE
CLIFTON SPRINGS, NY (opposite)

In the 19th century, Clifton Springs was slow to develop until Dr. Henry Foster began promoting his "water cure" in 1849. Many traveled hundreds of miles to be treated for various ailments in the town's natural sulfur springs.

ESPERANZA MANSION
BLUFF POINT, NY (above and opposite)

High on a bluff, Esperanza Mansion enjoys a spectacular, long view of Keuka Lake. John Nicholas Rose, a wealthy farmer in the nearby village of Penn Yan, built it in the mid-1800s. The mansion is a striking example of classical Greek Revival architecture and is a National Historic Landmark.

After a long, colorful past as a farm, vineyard, Underground Railroad link and county poorhouse, the 19th century mansion, faithfully restored to its original splendor, is now a full destination resort, complete with a fine dining restaurant and lodging in the mansion and the adjoining new Inn. The unique beauty of the mansion and its setting make it a popular venue for wedding receptions and other important events.

SOUTH MAIN STREET
GENEVA, NY (top and bottom)

Rising up a hillside from the northern shores of Seneca Lake, Geneva
is one of the oldest and most colorful communities in Ontario
County. Geneva's downtown area, with its century-old trees, stately
homes, historic Pulteney Square and sweeping views of the lake, has
been acclaimed as "the most beautiful street in America." Its striking
setting and old-world charm are reminiscent of the beauty of Geneva,
Switzerland.

88

HISTORIC MAIN STREET
SKANEATELES, NY (above)

Set on jewel-clear Skaneateles Lake, this quaint town shines brightly,
too. Fun to visit any time of year, Skaneateles' charming historic
downtown district is filled with fashionable shops, boutiques, restaurants, art galleries, and landmark buildings dating back to 1796.
During the winter holidays, downtown merchants don 19th century
costumes and re-create the magic of a Dickensian Christmas.

THE COMMONS
CORNING, NY (above)

Forty miles southwest of Ithaca, Corning is the home of the world-famous Steuben Glass factory. The charming, historic Market Street area flourishes with glass making studios, antique shops, restaurants and specialty shops.

NATIONAL CEMETERY
BATH, NY (top)

Some of the graves in this national cemetery, on the grounds of Bath's Veterans Administration Center, go back as far as the Civil War. The cemetery is one of over 120 national cemeteries that honor veterans of every war since the Revolutionary War.

VA MEDICAL CENTER
BATH, NY (bottom)

The Bath VA Medical Center began as a New York State Soldiers and Sailors Home in 1878. Today, it provides healthcare services to veterans from the Finger Lakes Region.

WOMEN'S RIGHTS NATIONAL HISTORIC PARK
SENECA FALLS, NY (above)

The first Women's Rights Convention in America was held in Seneca Falls in 1848. The park commemorates this historic meeting and women's continuing struggle for equal rights. The woman in the middle is Amelie Jenks Bloomer who is introducing Susan B. Anthony, on the left, to Elizabeth Cady Stanton for the first time.

TRINITY EPISCOPAL CHURCH
SENECA FALLS, NY (opposite)

This historic landmark next door to the Women's Rights Park, is easily one of the most photographed churches in the state, with its Late Gothic Revival architecture and authentic, Tiffany stained-glass windows.

BLUE WATER GRILL
SKANEATELES, NY (above)

This waterside eatery on Skaneateles Lake is a favorite with locals who enjoy a fun and casual atmosphere.

ICE FISHING ON CONESUS LAKE (opposite, top)

A hard freeze makes fishing a year-round sport on Conesus Lake, one of the six smaller Finger Lakes. Anglers drop a line in a small hole in the ice and enjoy the lake's world-famous abundance of bass, pike, walleye, perch, and bluegills.

ICE RACING ON WANETA LAKE (opposite, bottom)

Icy road conditions would keep most people indoors; however, icy lake conditions bring racing enthusiasts out in droves to test their winter driving skills. The Central New York Ice Racing Association supervises events on lakes that have at least 12-inches of ice and limits top speeds to 70 mph.

SHERWOOD INN
SKANEATELES, NY (top)

Built as a stagecoach stop in 1807, the Sherwood Inn has welcomed weary travelers for nearly two centuries. Painstakingly restored, the Inn today shines with fine, wood detailing, pegged wood floors, original fireplaces and antique furniture.

HISTORIC DOWNTOWN DISTRICT
SKANEATELES, NY (right)

Skaneateles is known for its scenic setting on Skaneateles Lake and its award-winning historic downtown. A walk down tree-lined streets takes you to historic homes and buildings and charming shops and restaurants.

THE THREE BEARS COURTHOUSE COMPLEX
OVID, NY (opposite)

The "Three Bears" nickname refers to a unique complex that features three "look alike" Greek-Revival Style buildings of descending size. Built in the mid-1800's, the complex is now a national historic landmark.

CAYUGA-SENECA CANAL, LOCK #2 (above)

Bring your own boat or join a tour and cruise the locks of the Cayuga & Seneca Canal 27 miles west to the Erie Canal. The Erie canal is a 524-mile waterway conneccting the Great Lakes to the Hudson River. The Cayuga-Seneca Canal runs through the quaint towns and villages of the Finger Lakes.

WATERFRONT MARINA
WATKINS GLEN, NY (opposite)

This marina at the south end of Seneca Lake is one of dozens that service Finger Lakes boaters. Seneca Lake is a perfect setting for water sports of all kinds—fishing, motor boating, sailing, and canoeing, to name a few.

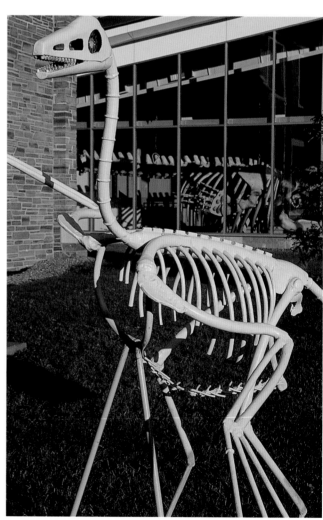

MUSEUM OF THE EARTH
ITHACA, NY (above and right)

Showcasing 360 natural history specimens of the world acclaimed collections of the Paleontological Research Institution, the new museum illustrates the 4.6 billion-year history of the Earth with a state-of-the-art hybrid of natural history, hands-on science and art exhibits. This architecturally acclaimed museum delights young and old with one of the nation's largest and finest fossil collections, which include many specimens from trilobites to mastodon and whale skeletons.

FIRST PRESBYTERIAN CHURCH
HECTOR, NY (oppositee)

Built in the late 1700s, this stately church is a national historic landmark and an outstanding example of the Federal-style architecture chosen by our country's founders to convey our new nation's image to the world.

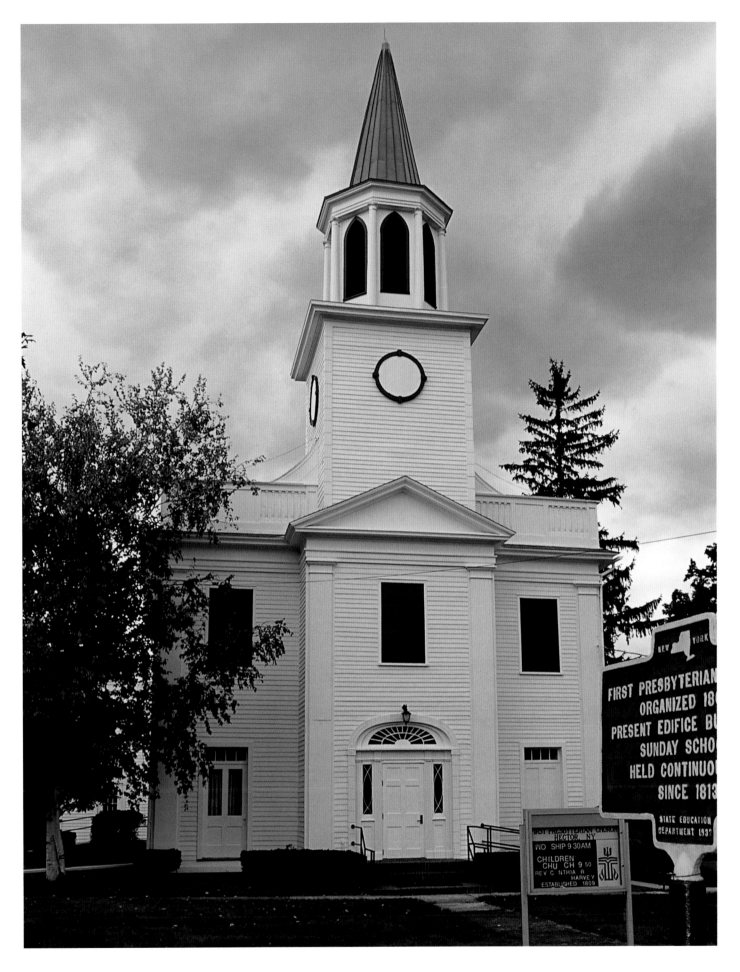

BIRKETT MILLS
PENN YAN, NY (above)

Founded in 1797, Birkett Mills is the world's largest producer of
buckwheat and buckwheat products. Visitors can tour the present
Mill which sits on the same site as the original stone mill, continuing
a tradition that is almost as old as America itself.

MEMORIAL TOWN HALL
NAPLES, NY (opposite)

The Naples Memorial Town Hall was erected in 1872 to honor the
more than 200 local men who served in the Civil War. Its history and
mid-19th century Italianate architecture have earned it a place on the
National Register of Historic Places.

CORNING MUSEUM OF GLASS
CORNING, NY (above)

After Hurricane Agnes nearly destroyed the museum and its priceless collections in 1972, the Museum rebounded in a brand new building safely above flood level. Designed by architect Gunnar Birkerts, the building's exterior rolls and flows like hot glass in a furnace and makes sharp right turns that represent glass' solid state. Today the museum showcases 35,000 glass items from ancient Egyptian times to modern day, including priceless pieces by Stueben Glass' founder, Frederick Carder, and Louis Comfort Tiffany.

COVERED BRIDGE
NEWFIELD, NY (above)

This charming, covered bridge in Newfield was lovingly restored by a nationally known preservationist in 1972. Popular in the 1800s because of plentiful lumber supplies, covered bridges or "timber tunnels" became popular places for social gatherings.

RACING AT THE GLEN
WATKINS GLEN, NY (above and opposite)

Racing began at "The Glen" in 1948 on a challenging course of asphalt, cement and dirt roads in and around the village of Watkins Glen. It was the first road race in the United States after World War II, and every year these unique antique cars let their engines roar again.

Since 1986, when the wildly popular NASCAR Winston Cup race returned to Watkins Glen, motor racing here has grown into New York State's largest weekend sporting event.

SIX MILE CREEK VINEYARD
ITHACA, NY (opposite)

Nestled on the southwest slope of one of Ithaca's most picturesque settings, Six Mile Creek Vineyards is a boutique winery that produces a variety of hand-crafted wines. The vineyard works with neighboring wineries to promote awareness of Finger Lakes wines.

SIX MILE CREEK VINEYARD
ITHACA, NY (top)

This vineyard's tasting room is housed in a restored, turn-of-the-century Dutch-reform barn. The panoramic view from the deck overlooks fields of grapevines that descend into the creek's gorge.

CONCORD GRAPES RIPENING
ITHACA, NY (bottom)

The red wines of the Finger Lakes region have enjoyed enthusiastic recognition over the last decade. Wine critics have called them "some of the most interesting wines sampled."

HUNT COUNTRY VINEYARDS
BRANCHPORT, NY (top)

The Denver Post called this winery "one of the loveliest wineries in the region." Visitors can tour on foot or ride on a hay wagon while enjoying the countryside of Keuka Lake.

BULLY HILL WINERY
HAMMONDSPORT, NY (bottom)

Bully Hill Vineyards' winemaking tradition stretches back to 1878 when the first of four generations of the Taylor family began growing grapes on the hill high above Keuka Lake. Taylor is the oldest family name to be continuously associated with wine and grapes in America.

SILVER THREAD WINERY
VALOIS, NY (oppposite)

Over two million wine aficionados and connoisseurs visit the numerous wineries in the Finger Lakes region every year, making it the state's second-largest tourist destination. Silver Thread Winery is an organic winery.

WINES OF THE FINGER LAKES (above)

Every season, the award-winning wines of the Finger Lakes earn more
national and international critical acclaim as they compete head-to-
head with wines from California's Napa Valley, Italy's Tuscany region,
and the wine-producing areas of France and Germany.

GREAT WESTERN WINERY
HAMMONDSPORT, NY (above)

Three major wineries, founded between 1860 and 1880, joined under one management team to form Great Western Winery, now a major vintner in the Finger Lakes. Located on the scenic southern end of Keuka Lake, the winery produces over 80 wines and sparkling wines under the Taylor, Great Western, GoldSeal and Henri Marchant labels. On site is a Visitor's Center and a Museum.

SEYVAL GRAPES RIPENING (above)

Many Finger Lakes wineries grow French-American hybrid grapes, such as the Seyval grape, to produce a variety of white wines that have helped elevate the region's reputation among wine connoisseurs.

DAWN OVER VINEYARDS
CAYWOOD, NY (opposite)

The Finger Lakes region offers everything from small-town beauty to the tranquility that can only be found in nature. Here, the dense vines, heavy with grapes, lie just under the morning mist.

DAWN OVER VINEYARDS
CAYWOOD, NY (top)

Wine connoisseurs who visit the wineries in Finger Lakes country
often compare the atmosphere to the excitement of California's Napa
Valley when it was first gaining international respect and recognition.

FOX RUN VINEYARDS
PENN YAN, NY (bottom)

Fox Run Vineyards is an active participant in the Finger Lakes'
"vinifera revolution." Their pure, European vinifera grapes growing
on the hillsides of Seneca Lake, are consistently producing award-
winning wines.

VINEYARD ON KEUKA LAKE (above)

Keuka Lake is one of the most pristine of the Finger Lakes. The grapes that grow on its lakeside slopes enjoy the same wine-producing climate as Germany and the Chablis region of France. The vineyards take advantage of the gravelly soil of the rolling hillsides and the microclimate of warm summer days and cool fall nights, moderated by the exceptionally deep lake waters.

HERON HILL WINERY
HAMMONDSPORT, NY (above)

One of the Finger Lakes's award-winning vinifera wineries, this Keuka
Lake vintner competes regularly nationally and internationally. Vini-
fera grapes are pure European grapes, not American or hybrid grapes.
Heron Hill is well known for its critically acclaimed Riesling wine.

GREAT WESTERN WINERY
HAMMONDSPORT, NY (above)

This internationally acclaimed winery has been producing fine wines since 1873 when its champagne took the first gold medal ever won by an American wine in foreign competition in Vienna, Austria. Since that impressive beginning, the winery has continued to grow in stature as well as size.

WIDMER WINERY
NAPLES, NY (above and opposite)

This historic winery had its beginnings in 1882 when Swiss winemaker John Jacob Widmer and his wife immigrated to the Finger Lakes, an area remarkably similar to European wine-making country. Visitors today can sample their wines in the cellar of their original homestead. Originally known for their fine Ports and Sherries, Widmer's product line is sold internationally and includes over 50 wines produced in facilities that combine Old World tradition with the latest technology.

GEESE LANDING
MONTEZUMA NATIONAL WILDLIFE REFUGE (top)

Montezuma's natural mix of wooded wetlands, marsh, and upland vegetation create a diverse wildlife community that features over 200 species of birds, and dozens of species of mammals, reptiles and amphibians.

GREAT BLUE HERON
MONTEZUMA NATIONAL WILDLIFE REFUGE (bottom and opposite)

The best known and most prolific of the herons, the Great Blue prefers solitude and nests in treetops.

GEESE LANDING
MONTEZUMA NATIONAL WILDLIFE REFUGE (above)

In the Spring, the skies and waters of Montezuma are filled with over
100,000 migrating geese and impressive flocks of snow geese, tundra
swans, mallards and black ducks. This wildlife refuge on Cayuga
Lake is the first "Important Bird Area" officially recognized in New
York State.

GREAT BLUE HERON
MONTEZUMA NATIONAL WILDLIFE REFUGE (opposite)

The great blue heron hunts for fish by day and by night, moving
slowly through shallow water or standing perfectly still until a fish
swims close enough to eat.

CANADA GEESE ON BEEBE LAKE
CORNELL UNIVERSITY CAMPUS (above)

Beebe Lake is a wonderful place for geese to raise a family. It is part of 3,500 acres of natural areas on and around the Cornell University campus that are managed and protected by the University's curator, Cornell Plantations. These ecologically fragile areas, obtained by gift and purchase, are protected for research, education, and the enjoyment of informed visitors.

CANADA GEESE FEEDING AT BEEBE LAKE
CORNELL UNIVERSITY CAMPUS (top)

These geese have it made! Not only can they swim and dine in
beautiful Beebe Lake, they enjoy great feeding on land, too.

SOLITARY VIREO SONGBIRD
FINGER LAKES NATIONAL FOREST (bottom)

Vireos are one of the most abundant songbirds in the deciduous
forests of the Finger Lakes region. Each male has a constant and
distinctive song that bonds them to their mate.

LUNA MOTH (above)

The Luna moth pauses long enough to show the photographer why it
is considered to be one of the Finger Lakes' most beautiful insects.
Graceful and fairylike, its sea-green wings span nearly five inches and
end in long flowing tails. Flying only at night, the luna moth loves to
eat hickory and walnut leaves and lives just one, brief week.